COMIC
CAPTIONED
CAPERS

OF LIL' JOHN AND COMPANY

COMIC CAPTIONED CAPERS

OF LIL' JOHN AND COMPANY

Clarence W. Dawson
author and photographer

SUNSTONE PRESS

SANTA FE
New Mexico

First Edition
Printed in the United States of America

10 9 8 7 6 5 4 3 2 1

_____

Library of Congress Cataloging in Publication Data:

Dawson, Clarence W., 1915-
    Comic captioned capers: of lil' John and company / Clarence W. Dawson, author
and photographer.—1st ed.
        p. cm.
    ISBN: 0-86534-232-6 (pbk.) : $8.95
    1. Family —Humor.
PS3554.A9474C66   1995
813' .54—dc20   94-23694
                                                  CIP

Published by SUNSTONE PRESS
              Post Office Box 2321
              Santa Fe, NM 87504-2321 / USA
              (505) 988-4418 / orders only (800) 243-5644
               FAX (505) 988-1025

Dedicated
to the memory
of my precious wife,
Eddie Mae Hurley Dawson

Writer-Photographer Dawson

Mr. Dawson is the author of three novels, *Return of Montezuma, Beebuzzards Atop the Cacass,* and *Desert Vendetta,* as well as an inspirational book, *Everybody Needs a Little John* (referring to his son).

Dawson, who obtained B.A. and M.A. degrees from Hardin-Simmons University, is also the author of 31 magazine and Sunday supplement features, many of which have been illustrated by his photos.

He has majors in English, Spanish, and journalism, subjects he taught in three high schools during his teaching tenure of 44 years. Among honors he achieved while working in the latter field was his being acclaimed Texas' Outstanding Journalism Teacher of the Year (1969) and his being inducted in 1976 into The Order of the Golden Quill.

A native of Minden, Louisiana, he has attended seven universities/colleges, including three in Old Mexico. An ardent aficionado of this country, Dawson lived with Mexican families during his studies there, learning more about Hispanic culture, reflected in his writings.

As an athlete at the Las Cruces (New Mexico) high school, he lettered in track, excelled in intramural boxing competition, and later was lightweight representative of the New Mexico State College Boxing Team, winning distinction in an All-Southwest Boxing Tournament hosted by the New Mexico Military Academy, in Roswell.

President of the Las Cruces Methodist Young Peoples Department in 1936, he was also chief executive of the Cliff Dwellers, A Methodist organization comprised of teenagers representing New Mexico and Texas.

Forward

The chief character of this book was also the principal subject of one of his father's earlier works, *Everybody Needs a Little John,* a true narrative which also contains some amusing captioned photos of John, his relatives, friends and pets.

The latter presents John—as this book does—from his diaper days though his early childhood.

Born in 1970, he is now married to the former Anita Egan and the couple reside in Nacogdoches, Texas.

John still shares his father's grief over the 1988 death of Eddie Mae, their devoted mother and wife.

John has one nephew and five nieces. Angie McGuyer, the oldest niece, is just one year younger than her uncle.

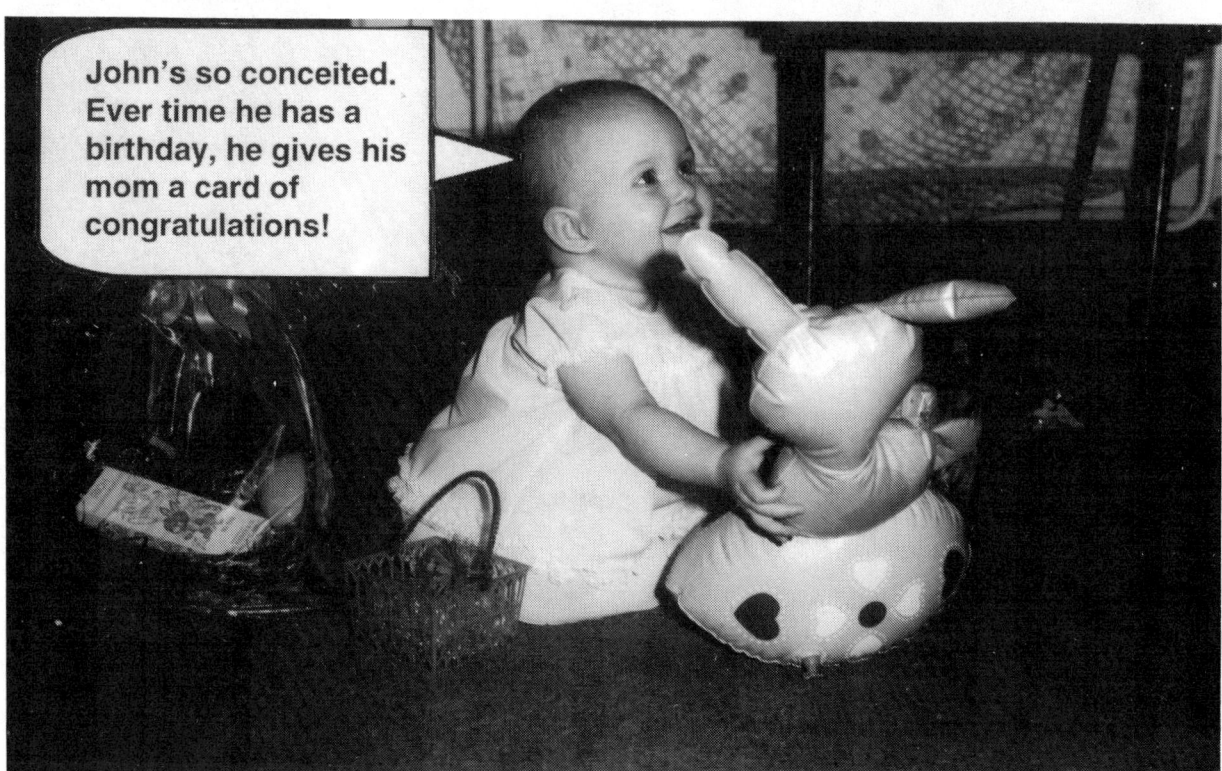

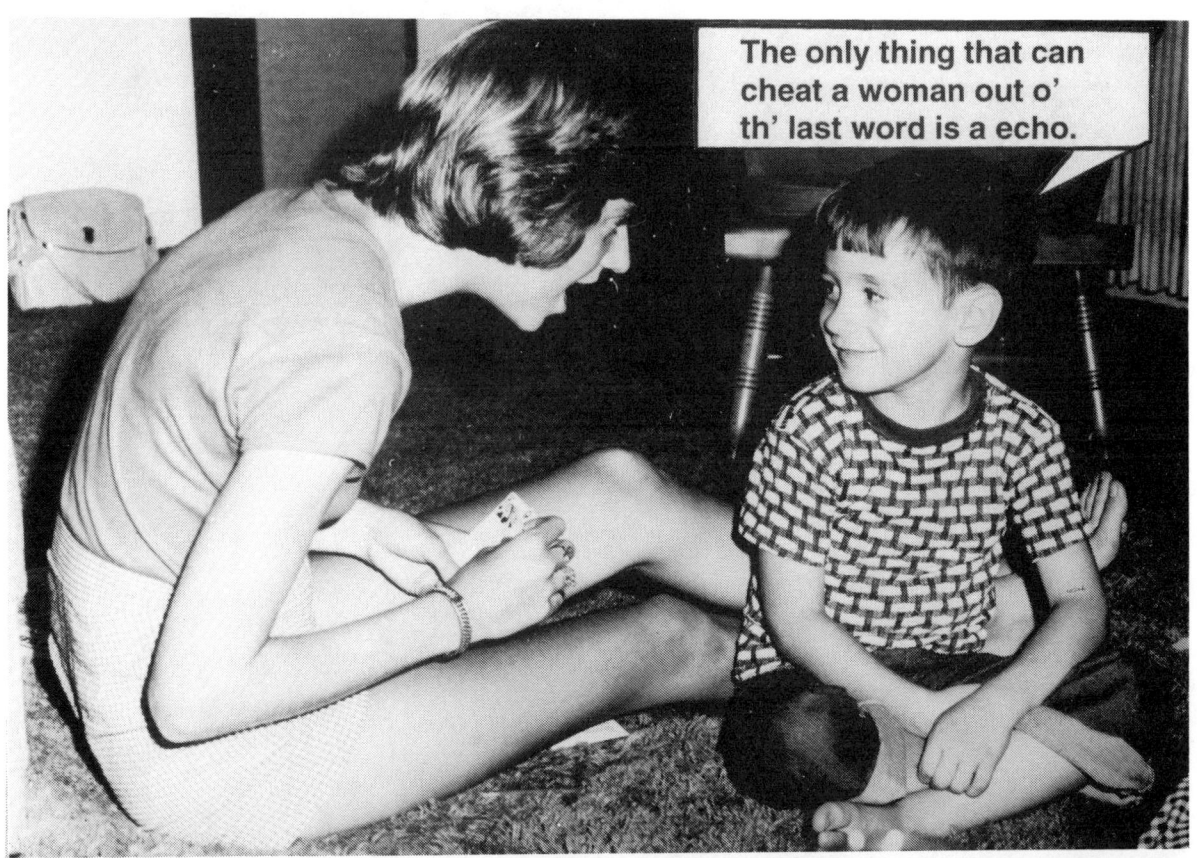

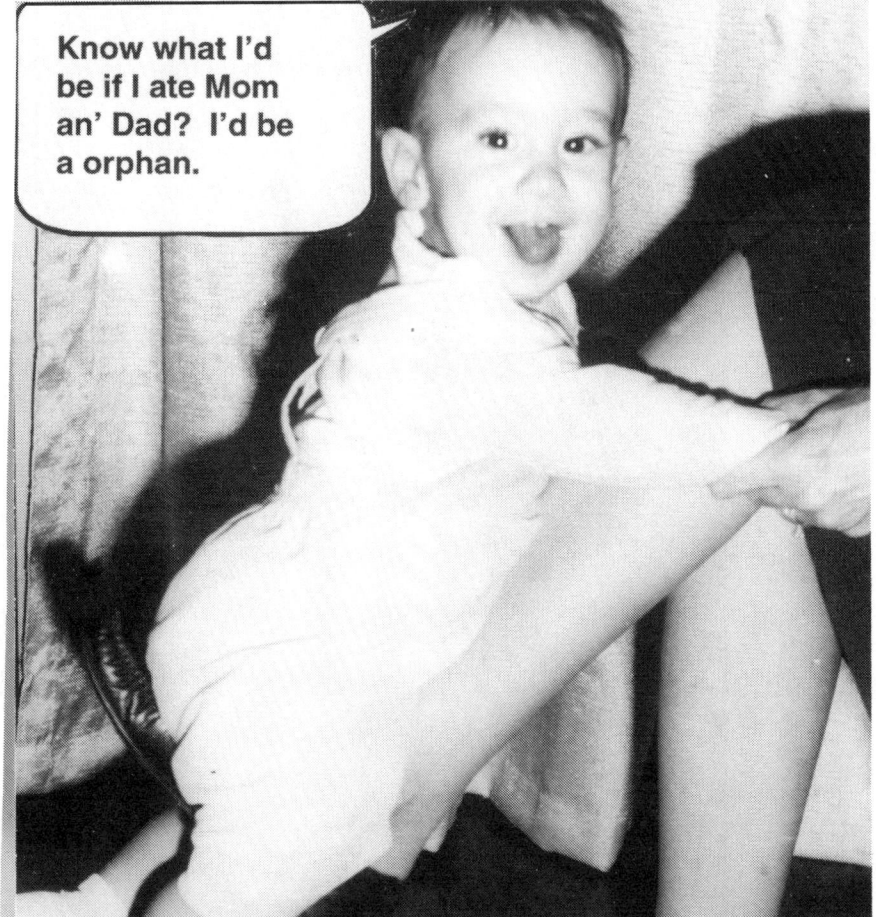

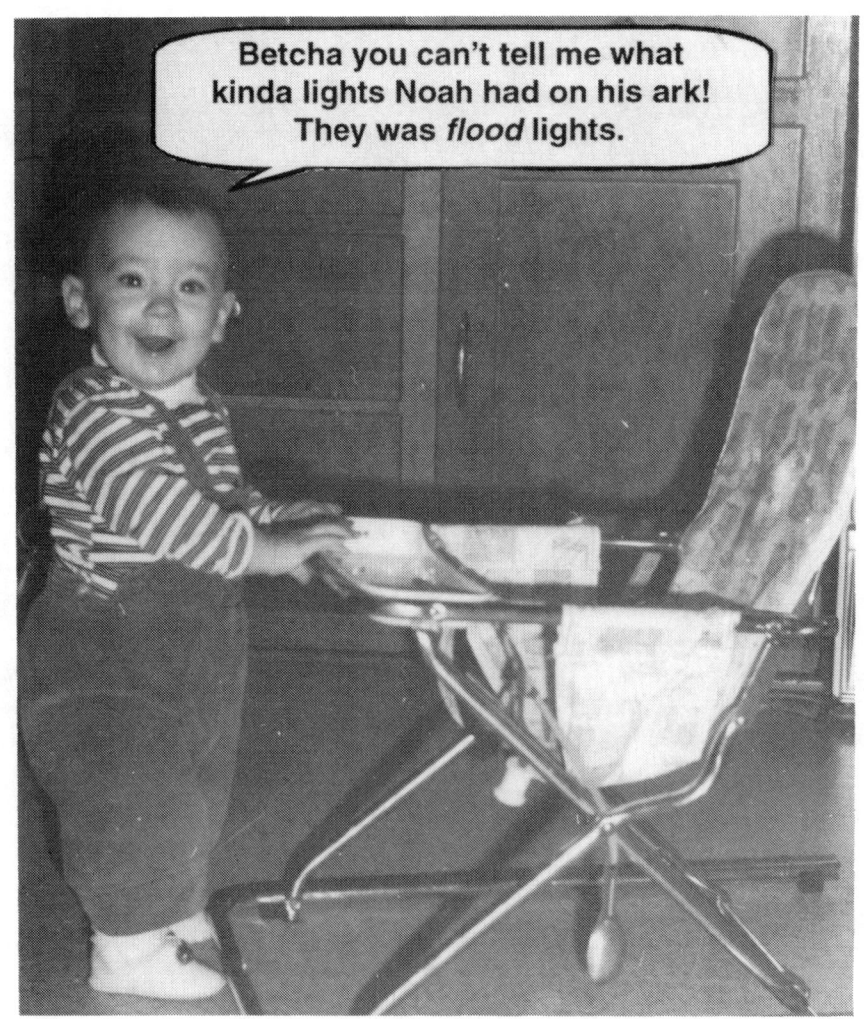

48